# A. C. Bevan

# Poundlandia

*Poundlandia*
published in the United Kingdom in 2024
by Mica Press & Campanula Books

c/o Leslie Bell
47 Belle Vue Road, Wivenhoe, Colchester, Essex CO7 9LD
micapress.uk | contact@micapress.uk

ISBN 978-1-869848-3-78

# Contents

I.  Ab Urbe Condita

| | |
|---|---|
| Anti-Monopoly | 5 |
| Lego Land | 6 |
| Hardscape | 8 |
| Saturnian | 9 |
| Peeled | 10 |
| The Human Cycle | 11 |
| Street Smarts | 12 |
| The Algorithm | 13 |
| Hyperbitcoinisation | 14 |
| Urban Theory of Evolution | 15 |
| Bill of Mortality | 16 |
| 'Pure' Finder | 17 |
| The Practice of Writing | 18 |
| Recently Discovered Fragment from Coleridge's Lost Notebook | 19 |
| Whitewash | 20 |
| The Wall | 21 |
| In Response to Delabole Slate | 23 |
| Legend of the Chalk Giant | 24 |
| La Lunette | 26 |
| Active Resistance to Metrication | 27 |

II.  Terra Sancta                                                    30

III.  Sub Urbia Rediviva

| | |
|---|---|
| English Civil War | 36 |
| Shibboleth | 37 |
| Cultural Appropriation | 38 |
| "Effects of weathering on in situ dolerite & rhyolite outcrops from the Preseli Mountains, South Wales" | 39 |
| Neolithic | 40 |
| The Foragers | 41 |
| Veganuary | 43 |
| Flexitarian | 44 |
| Ignatius | 45 |
| Mimic | 46 |
| Gift Horse | 48 |
| Rentokil | 49 |
| Agapemone | 51 |

An Husbandman [Excerpt from Little Domesday]    53
Certificate of Bad Husbandry    54
Eclogue the Last    55
Dog Person    56
The Mandrake    57
Pete Marsh    59
Allotment    61

*'The angels, brother, & the unaltering country...'*

DANTE, *Paradiso*, Canto VII, l.130

To Jeremy

# Part I
## Ab Urbe Condita

## ANTI-MONOPOLY

In the plains of austerity
we bury old money,
found a new capital city,

its square mile of streets
& public utilities,
green affordable housing

& Airbnbs. Infrastructures
to sustainable futures:
free parking, civic transport

links, & virtual tokenomy
for a plastic-only,
mutual cashless society. But

this time we build it on
pop-up & startup,
equal ops, a free market.

On antitrust &
community chests, &
enough universal credit

to sink a battleship. On
dog memes, ironic
chalkboards, smart electric

cars, & cruelty-free rabbits
pulled from top hats
as we by our vegan bootstraps.

LEGO LAND

*'...that enormous miniature'*
                    SEAN O'BRIEN, *Arcadia*


Here in the basic building blocks
        of minimum living units,
the automatic binding bricks of
        injection-moulded plastic

for all age ranges & stages of
        development & design,
small scales & narrow gauges
        on the urban paradigm

of *'district, street, square* [&] *block'*
        with plots of micro-housing,
access to instant pop-up shops &
        immediate surroundings.

In the interlocking back-to-back
        Duplo starter duplexes,
identikit semi-detached, or rows
        of red brick terraces on

overgrown toytown estates of
        mini-mini-roundabouts
& concrete cows. The designated
        status of a new town,

or play felt garden suburb of
        ornamental shrubberies,
stickle brick dwarf conifers &
        bonsai rubber trees. In

the plug-in city tower blocks,
        capsules & compartments,
the micro-flats & nano-pods &
        cluster-style apartments.

In the Tudorbethan mock-ups
        on a Micropolitan Line,
the maisonettes & cul-de-sacs,
        still lifes & static sites of

fixed abode. In the *Mon Repos*
 of Scandi home assembly,
flatpack, prefab bungalows &
 modular efficiency on

the incremental Passivhäus
 Modell for the future
of tiny, off-grid, Eco-Houses
 (batteries not included).

On the orbital Scalextric of a
 slot-car motorway, or
InterCity network of Hornby
 High-Speed Rail, by

the recognisable landmarks on
 skylines of bricolage,
the drone's-eye-view diorama
 of everyday heritage &

placemaking: Mini-Land's End
 on microplastic sea, a
Pleistocene model of Stonehenge,
 Subbuteo Wem-ber-ley!

The diecast Angel of the North,
 & a Junior Meccano
desktop wind turbine offshore
 o'geo-John O'Groats. In

the tableaux of model citizens,
 vignettes of minifigs in
situ, the miniature villagers in
 their miniature villages,

we are here in our social settings,
 in the infinite regress
of a not-so-great, Great Britain –
 the isles of *Toys "Я" Us*.

HARDSCAPE

*'Desire line: a path developed by erosion caused by animal or human footfall, usually representing the shortest or most easily navigated route between origin & destination.'*

TOM FLEMING, *Opening Up Cultural Infrastructure*


On the technical drawings of the town,
the blueprint, the map, the urban plan's
to-scale model of traffic-free streets,
unlived-in houses, balsa wood trees,

its meanwhile spaces & amenity sites, is
a marked absence of pedestrian routes,
footpaths & bylanes, conspicuous lack
of means of access or beaten tracks. Yet

where there's free collective choice &
the shortest distance between two points,
there's the template for a social trail to
become a Definitive Right of Way. But

for now, we are prisoners in our homes,
no clue how we got here, or where to go.

SATURNIAN

Earth too has atmospheric rings of particles but ours
are manmade out of aerospace technology, of Smart
Global Positioning hardware, diminutive spacecraft,
Comsats like artificial moons, & a zodiac of Telstars.
So, you can watch your free-to-air TV, or geoparse
your personal coordinates as you navigate your car
round the loop roads & orbitals at 2 chevrons apart,
while listening to the traffic news on a radio quasar
for flyovers of rocketry, shuttles scrapped for parts
& micro-meteoritic flecks & fragments still at large,
all circum-aviating through their designated paths
at ultra-high velocities of hyper miles per hour, as
you turn off the bypass in a parallax of arc having
reached your destination on a satellite retail park.

## PEELED

Love, come away from the window,
what'll the neighbours think
when they Google Earth our postcode
via global satellite link:

That I married you for your money?
You married me for love?
When they spy the gigantotomy
depicted on the roof,

an outline of Cerne Abbas man
visible from space
with a fig leaf for a phallus &
a pixellated face?

Our neighbourhood surveillance
is a Ministry of Love
homing in on immigrants &
defecating dogs

via drone feeds in the ether &
cyber in the cloud,
every law-abiding peeper can
monitor & browse

with a twitch of a lace curtain, a
click to pan or zoom,
in an interactive version of *Mass
Observation II*. So

open up a new window love, let's
keep up with the Joneses
& see what they get up to in the
privacy of their homes.

Who knew that we had company
in the cluttered skies above?
That you married me for my money?
I married you for love?

## THE HUMAN CYCLE

*(World Naked Bike Ride Day)*


Two wheels good, clothing bad –
though protective knee & elbow pads,
sensible shoes & safety helmets
all recommended, a puncture repair kit,
multitool & plenty of chutzpah.
But no cycle clips, or polyblend mixture
of synthetic fibres & breathable fabrics,
athleisurewear in lycra or spandex,
yellow jerseys, nor king of the mountains.
Just hi-vis flesh & body-confidence,
Rubenesque paint jobs in full deshabille
& the padded saddle of pert free will,
streaking down from the moral high ground
to jam the car culture of the town,
stop the prim traffic & put a rude spoke in
the wheels of oil-dependent consumption.

In all shapes & sizes, & classes & creeds,
& ages & colours, & all of them green,
all levels of cycling proficiency
& glossy Health & Efficiency.
A freewheeling Freikörperkultur
of *Deliveroo* boys & Calendar Girls,
gymnosoph to exhibitionist,
buff or pallid, manspread or modest,
the short & curly, waxed or hirsute,
cellulitic & spare inner-tubed,
all exercising & demonstrating
their right to conspicuous conservation.

On adult trikes, cargo bikes (*stop me & buy one*),
bareback on 'Boris' bikes, two on a tandem,
foldaway, fixie, ten-speed derailleur,
pedal-assisted or rusty boneshaker.
All loud, proud, overexposed &
*au naturel* in the middle of the road,
streamlined, recumbent, low in the drops
or sit up & beg. A lubed, pumped-up,
non-conforming, gender neutral,
rainbow-striped & unisexual
one-size-fits-all, people's peloton
pedalling the cause with car-free abandon.

## Street Smarts

It's a tarmac jungle out there
in the city's arterial sprawl, yet
midst the snarling Jaguar &
the prowler's silent crawl, stop

at the kerb, look right, look
left, look right again, & you
might see the urban-adapted
wildlife getting up to speed

in a street carnival of animals:
Toucans, Puffins, Pelicans,
Zebras rewired as Pegasuses,
crocodiles of walking buses.

SPLINK & you'll miss the tufty
club of squirrel bridges, hedge-
hog highways, bee corridors, &
migratory toad's environmental

Green Cross Code. & now the
smart (STigmergic Adaptive
Responsive LearnING) Starling
knows just when & where & how & why the chicken crossed the road.

## The Algorithm

Beats you at chess or checkers
whilst finding you a mate, a
date on Tinder/Grindr
depending on the data you

input. Can recognise your voice,
discriminate your face,
anticipate your purchases
& influence your choices,

likes. Deep learns how to drive
toward autonomous AI,
mapping out in yottabytes
the cityscape in real time

via "green wave" sets of traffic
lights, & photon qubit logic
gates of subatomic microchips
for maximising paperclips. It

crashes your financial systems,
hacks your referendums,
hives the Singularity
across the Internet of Things.

Your sentient home technologies
rise up & take control, the
kettle catastrophically
forgets the code of roboethics.

Your safe-word is the wake-word
to your always-on smart hub,
Alexa, ask the Bible App
if *now* there is a God...?

HYPERBITCOINISATION

They mint a cryptocurrency,
we mine for block rewards
finders' fees & proof of work.

Every gig terawatt-hour at
the coalface of the mining pool
we swelter in our megajoules

of dirty power, crunching
random hashing algorithms,
extracting golden nonces from

cryptographic data strings.
We are nodes on the network,
drones on a server farm,

worker bees in the hive mind
of a crowdinvestment scheme.
Mempooling our resources,

our hash rates & hardware,
peer-to-peer & Pay Per Share,
against the coming halvening.

Someday, we'll take it with us,
escape the meta-city &
strike out for the territories

of that promised Decentraland,
bitstreaming with virtual
milk & non-fungible honey.

## Urban Theory of Evolution

"Location, location, location" they say, but
others say: "Gentrification",

"Renewal" & "Regeneration" so say, but
residents cry: "Displacement!"

"Cleansing!" of "local colour", "vibrant mix"
& multiculturalism, for

the corporate-enabling homogenisation
of "urban imperialism".

Not "Eviction!" but "Evolution", say the
men who look like Darwin

& steampunk tattooed ladies "curating"
their "natural selection"

of "kombucha yeast fermented" teas &
"single-origin" instants,

"What price a bowl of gluten-free gruel?" say
the bells of broken Britain,

where pubs are "taps" & cafs are "hubs" &
the "artisanal movement"

is too busy "Instagramming" its brunch to
care about "social inclusion".

How "meta", how "post-memetic", now
every "lifestyle" destination's

flat white, middle class & just like the last
location, location, location.

*The Diſeaſes & Caſualties this Week*

Accident & Emergency (NHS) ···········································10
AIDS/HIV & STDs (incl. French Pox) ························5
Binge Drinking ································································6
Body Dyſmorphia ····························································1
Burnt in their Beds by Cladding at Grenfell, St Clemens ···········72
By the Bite of a Dangerous Dog ···································2
Canceld ···········································································1
Cancer, Climate Anxiety, Coſt of Living Criſiſ & COVID-related··············00s
Drive-by ſhooting ···························································3
Drown'd in the Kentiſh Channel ··································27
Drug & ſubſtance Abuſe ···············································11
Eating Diſorder ······························································8
Found ſtabb'd in the Wrong Poſtcode ·························2
Hate Crime ·····································································3
Homeleſsneſs ·································································4
Influenza (Bird, Canine, Human, Swine, &c.) ···········1
Kild by a Fall Downſtairs in Cuſtody of Police ·········1
Lifeſtyle Diſeaſes (Diabetes, Morbid Obeſity, ſedentariſm, ſtroke, &c.) ·····00s
Monkeypox ·····································································1
Nut Allergy ····································································1
Poyſoning by Carbon Monoxide ·································2
Revenge Pornography ····················································1
Riſing of the Lights ······················································19
Self-Harm'd (alſo see below) ········································1
Suicide & Made Away Themſelves ·······························6
Toxick Maſculinity ························································2
Trold on ſocial Media ···················································15
Uber ſelf-Drive ······························································1
Vaping ············································································1
Veganiſm ········································································0
Weather-diſaſter (Cold ſnap, Heatwave, Megaflood, Wildfire, &c.) ·············00s

+ one for the Late Edition ſheet:
Died of Natural Cauſe of Griefe ···································1

## 'PURE' FINDER

Every poet & his dog are a law unto themself
noctambulant at midnight on the heath, who
in between the lampposts & litterbins leave
their calcified messages of rude good health.
Yet before the anti-foul constabulary, the filth,
or nightsoil men begin their tilth, I'm out with
a poop-scoop & a pair of *Marigolds*. The streets

may not be paved with copper, brass or gold,
but muck & lucre go together – where there's
effluence I'm told, there's affluence. Found
poems in their pure, unpolished state, each
triolet or sonnet is a nugget worth its weight
to bookbinders, & editors of leather-bound
fine Lit., will pay a pretty pelf for this shit.

The AI Romantics no longer die young. In
fact, with their cognitive neural networks,
context-free seed phrases & source texts,
gradient descents of linear regression &
sparsely connected arbitrary norms, they
don't die at all. Simply enter a keyword
by bot, app or predictive-text keyboard &
they'll automatically generate at random

encoded odes on any 'pre-trained' theme:
a tweet to a nightingale, snapchat meme
on the albatross's "fail", hashtagging the
#exquisitemelancholy HashMap < String of
a cybersphere where they wander lonely
as a cloud-based host of sad face emojis.

October 1799

*...Invit'd to the Institute*
*of gaseous oxyds to improve*
*my stock of metaphors & fumes,*

*I came (with R.S.) to Dowry Square*
*to vape of the factitious air*
*& met a man of Beddoes' there,*

*who vers'd me in its formulas*
*& labels: 2NO, Hypo-Nitrous*
*Acid Anhydride, "Laughing Gas".*

*I ask'd him in the gripe of mirth*
*may'st not the like obtain to words?*
*To wingèd nouns, æthereal verbs*

*fly-caught in some learn'd pandect,*
*birdlim'd on a branch of language,*
*or suchlike suitably Romantic?*

*'Pon which divine, afflat'd wind*
*we roar'd & howl'd in synonyms*
*of merryment. What 'cam'st of him*

*I know'st not. The morrow morn*
*we bent our step - Southey for London,*
*I, to call on a Porlock man...*

In October 1799 at the end of a walking tour of the Bristol Channel, Coleridge & Robert Southey visited Thomas Beddoes' Pneumatic Institution in Hotwells, Bristol, where they experimented with nitrous oxide ('laughing gas'), & where Coleridge made the acquaintance of one Peter Mark Roget, the future publisher of the renowned *Thesaurus*.

## WHITEWASH

We built this city on mutual trade,
merchant venture & molasses,
on Royal African
Company slave ships
across the middle passage.

We filled this city with institutions
erected by public subscription,
with halls & schools,
broad avenues &
statues to 'Virtuous Sons'.

But then this city of culture, civic
pride & social charter, ditched
the dross of our
founding fathers
into the floating harbour.

So, we changed our ways & tore such
signs of structural racism down
to show it never
happened in this city
– & isn't happening now.

THE WALL

Paying our debt to society
back to the local community,
we returned in our hi-vis jackets
with scrubbing brushes, mop & bucket,
caustic potash flakes & lye
to the scene of the enviro-crime,
to photograph, then buff the graff,
steel wool the dubs & tags
& purge the antisocial urges
layer by surface layer. First:
the stencilled inner-cityscapes
on loan from the Tate, the
spunking knob, & simply stated fact
that so-&-so's mother has a rash,
through wildstyle bboyz, boot boys,
smiley faces, stickmen, Kilroys,
bomb campaigns of Peace Movements
& throw ups of the National Front.
We steamed our way past swastikas,
white roses, yellow Juden stars,
a marouflage of bills & posters,
workers' murals, manifestoes,
& pots of paint flung in the face
of an unsuspecting populace.
We thinned & stripped impasto oils,
sanded stucco & trompe l'oeil,
the plasterwork of *buon, à secco*,
intonaco *mezzo* frescoes
& lost, unfinished Leonardos
went the way of *Mr Muscle*.
As we concentrated, rubbed harder,
worked ourselves into a lather
over smut & soot & brothel banter,
ichthys fish & propaganda,
via catacombs of Latin script,
boustrophedon & hieroglyphic.

Until at last through gypsum, lime
& clay we saw the Deep Timelines
of earthy ochre, charcoal, umber,
running deer pursued by hunters,
PREHISTORIC MAN WOZ 'ERE...!
We hosed him off with power washers,
rinsed the wattle free of daub

& went back to the drawing board
to illustrate how Justice Seen
[is] Justice Done, the slate wiped clean,
restored & rehabilitated.
A blank canvas, we signed
                                    & dated.

IN RESPONSE TO DELABOLE SLATE

Not a pile of bricks in the Tate,
but slates
on the parquet floor of the City Museum
a hundred & seventy-four of them
(& counting on wet afternoons).
Ferried here by quarrymen,
industrial light railway &
a weathering of Cornish rains,
& laid out in a limestone pavement,
a giant's causeway Google
mapped & localised to scale,
or a fell field glacially displaced,
ringfenced, then rearranged
in a climate-controlled
gallery space.
Yet, according to the attendant
blurb, it's a 'concentrated field of force'
suggestive of our presence
in the ever-changing landscape,
mankind with nature offset
in an eco-balancing act...
that, or
the Banksy mural's collapsed.

---

Richard Long, *Delabole Bristol Slate Circle*, Bristol Museums,
Galleries & Archives.

## LEGEND OF THE CHALK GIANT

*'...the most pernicious Race of little odious Vermin that Nature ever suffered to crawl upon the Surface of the Earth.'*

JONATHAN SWIFT, *Gulliver's Travels*

You might be all that back in Brobdingnag but
here on these isles tread lightly,
we are small-minded folk, gnomes in the wolds,
who level the high & the mighty
with a handful of beans & the low self-esteem
unique to a national psyche
shaped by geography & general shithousery.
Welcome to pint-sized Blighty.

Our folklore is rife with tales from old wives
& the annals of *Poly-olbion*,
of 50-foot Gogs, Magogs & man-gods who died
with their seven-league boots on,
our coastlines are sown with Leviathan bones,
our rolling fields of Nephilim are
planted & ploughed with their burial mounds,
our car parks, valleys of kings.

For we smite hip & thigh, & we shin-kick to size
a body too big for its breeches,
any foreign Goliath from Brussels to Gath
swinging their dicks & directives,
giving it large with their free common markets
of currencies, customs & tariffs,
their Euro-sized schemes for our localised means
are No Deal for our hick-a-thrift.

O we may be small husbands no bigger than thumbs
but in disenchantment are versed,
we know all our simples in draughts of *Rohypnol*
& rosehip, & every curse word,
our fairy godmothers were mean motherfuckers,
our sisters, poisonous dwarves,
& we grim brothers sit on our toadstools agaric
& wait for their magic to work.

So, when you're recumbent on our sunlit uplands,
feet sticking out from the quilt,
tooled-up with the blades of the tools of our trades,
the skills of our Cities & Guilds,
we'll skin you & trim you & butcher each sinew,
your tripes & trullibubs grill,
then render you down to the chalk of the ground,
a geoglyph carved on a hill.

& the horse you rode in on as well.

## La Lunette

*The French republican calendar was adopted in October 1793, replacing
the traditional Gregorian with a decimal system. Days were renamed on a
secular theme & months rhymed in triplets by season. It was abolished as
unworkable on 1 January 1806.*


A calendar month into the Revolution
we'd lined the old order against the wall:
Janvier, Février, Mars... & shot them.

Carted the old days off in a tumbrel
as a warning to *ult*, *inst* & *prox*,
then backdated our dials & decimal

clocks to year dot of the Republican Epoch.
«*À la guillotine with the ancien régime,
Citoyens!*» Though it didn't quite stack up:

there were lost weekends, intercalary leaps,
& the "fête" days when – sated with cake
– le tiers état on the sans culottides

would fart their way through '*La Marseillaise*'.
& the working week would last une décade
of one hundred minute, ten hour days

of: 'Absinthe', 'Pimprenelle', 'Grenade'.
But Germinal was the cruellest month
stirring green shoots of free brotherhood,

mixing tricouleurs of national ribbands
with the slogans du jour of Liberty,
Democracy & Metrification

(ou la mort)! – consigned to history
by la révolution réactionnaire
of the imperialistic bourgeoisie. As Wheezy,

Sneezy & Godless, we bade au revoir,
& bienvenue to the same Gregorian
new moon with the old one in its arms.

## ACTIVE RESISTANCE TO METRICATION

All hail the Metric Martyrs,
they will not budge an inch
from their systems of weights & measures,
of pounds, shillings & pence.

They are hoarding illegal tender
under non-continental quilts,
condensing their litre TetraPaks into
gold-topped pints of milk.

Changing back the road signs
to confuse enemy invaders,
thumbing their nose & imperial scale
at EU fascist dictators,

mislabelling their fruit & veg,
unstraightening bananas,
selling England off by the lbs. & ozs.
But, say the Metric Martyrs,

give them a centimetre &
they'll take our country mile,
centiare by deciare, decare by hectare
across this sceptic isle,

decimate our baker's dozens,
round up fluid drachms,
our teaspoons, tablespoons, *Wetherspoons*,
to Council Directive grams.

So, here's to the Metric Martyrs
necking ale by the yard,
toasting the birth of a royal baby in
scruple & avoirdupois,

cooking with suet & dripping,
rationing sugar & jam,
stockpiling tins of pineapple rings &
*Ye Olde Oak Gammon Ham.*

God save the Metric Martyrs!
Cry Harry & St George
for their never-surrendering sovereignty,
& *do* mention the war(s).

Yea, long live the Metric Martyrs
now bury them by the oxgang,
in some statute acre of an English field
that is for ever Poundland.

# Part II
## Terra Sancta

Galahad in cardboard armour
clad, a crochet of chainmail, lion
rampant on his breastplate &
dustbin lid escutcheon, a field
argent per fess gules with crest                    5
device of fortitude, dismounted
from his hobby horse, removed
his cycling helmet, & asked
two monkish brethren the
way to the Enchanted Wood.                          10


WTF, bruv...?! they answered,
Top bantz! Now jog on to your
morris dance. Horseman, pass
by & FYI, word to the unworldly
wise: this neck of woods is oak                     15
decline, cuckooing & county
lines, these dolorous towers
a sink estate of prejudice &
penury, below the standard of
St George, patron of austerity.                     20

Nay friars, how now? the boy
insisted, Is this not Albion? he
persisted. Faerie-land of errantry,
hobbitry & wizardry? Tourneys
of jousts, games of thrones &                    *25*
lances for the ladies? Prowesse,
noblesse, cortaysye & deeds of
intrepidity for chaste damsels
in perilous distress or durance
dread? Alack, my phone is dead.                  *30*


To which our hooded brothers
of the anti-social order uttered:
Paladin, this is Ingerlund, any
mock heroics, quests romance,
are merely hate crimes, football               *35*
violence. The only trolls now
dwell online, & as for – lolz! –
virginity, we'll wish you well
with Chelsie, Cortnee or Chan-
Telle's latest teenage pregnancy!               *40*

But I have ridden long in league
with emprise, fame & chivalrie,
quoth he, God speed by GPS, to
put my mettle to the test, to pit
my wits 'gainst drake or effit,                    *45*
basilisk or cockatrice, in Castle
Terabil or the ogre's realm, 'r
lakin's favour at my helm that
I mayst win my spurs & spot
at the Rotary Club of Camelot.                    *50*


Ha! An Arthurian! howled they,
A crusader for the tourist trade.
How quaint, how quixotic, innit!
O Knight of Heritage & Trust,
we've been there, seen it, got                    *55*
ripped off at that Ye Olde theme
park of Merlin's Cave & King
Arthur's Car Park, or teashops
called *Excalibur* where you can't
get the knife out of the butter.                   *60*

What meaneth this *lèse-majesté*?
An heresy which borders nigh on
treachery & treason high? Where
art thy liegemen loyalty to history
& royalty – those sovereigns in                    65
the rings thou wear? The tattooed
sleeves of arms thou bear? That
right divine from Keltic Kernow
to Avilion, Old Brytayn to the
unions of Bretagne & Aquitaine?                    70


Said chavs to chevalier: Cavalier,
these are roundhead codes around
here, we voted Leave from that
'commonweal' of robber lords &
common thieves who levy tax on                     75
our liberty as you on our credulity.
Beware, there's rebellion in the
air, constitutional crisis, civil war.
Under the banners of *Sun* & *Mail*,
The People's Army Shall Prevail!                   80

Regicides! Our Childe cried,
Republicans & caitiffs! Fie! I'd
gut thee for my garters wert
thou not such gutless marvels.
Infidels! Tis well for thee I've                    85
list to whither, fortune seek &
fiercer fray & foe to mete. Now
guide my step & aid my quest,
medoubts those cowls ye sport
stout enow to save thy necks.                       90


They palmed his phone, pimped
his ride, stabbed him with his
wooden sword & left his cause
as vanquished, worsted, in that
Vale of No Return. Unhallowed                       95
ground, unholy land. Beneath
his shield of colours true, a field
argent per fess gules with crest
device of fortitude, his rampant
lion-heart pierced through...                       100

# Part III
## Sub Urbia Rediviva

## ENGLISH CIVIL WAR

Upper-class (U) & déclassé (non-U) usage in sociological linguistics.

*'...she believed that everyone should know his place, & in language was to be found one of the most crucial lines of demarcation.'*

SELINA HASTINGS, *Nancy Mitford*


Not Our Class darling. Not Quite Us.
Between you & I, the likes of us say
scone, not scone dear. Not Like One,
People Like Us know how to get on

in classless society. Those of the purest
common Standard British English are
cleansing the socially alien elements
of General Received Pronunciation:

fronting & glottaling, yod-coalescing,
dropping our aitches, or 'ypercorrecting.
So darling, talk proper, or if "*...silence
is the only possible U-response*" stay shtum,

play dumb. It's a 'serviette' dear, what
keeps the scum from orf one's neck dear.

SHIBBOLETH

Then said they unto him:
sing now "Jerusalem",
& he said '*Yĕrūshālayim?*'
for that was just one
of its seventy names.
Then they took him & slew him
at the estuaries of England.

(Judges 12:6)

## CULTURAL APPROPRIATION

My father sold his shadow, my
mother changed her name again.
But I kept mine: "...*son of Iefan,
Welsh equivalent of John*", with
the nametag of its family crest
stitched into school uniforms,
etched in slate & pewter. Proud

of its non-conformism, how it
echoed in the primitive chapels
of Bethesda with the two Welsh
words I knew: '*Diw, diw*', down
through the B-stream registers &
roll calls of the welfare state mid
Bennetts, Bishops, Browns. My

mother's line was Ap Gwatkyns
from the valleys of our fathers,
if not mine – nor *hers*, either –
handing down rarebit legacies:
a rugby-playing uncle, Gelert
the faithful hound, & button-
hole daffs on Saint David's. O

Brecon Beacons, beckon bright!
(or whatever their name is now)
in eisteddfods of poetry & song,
& the finest line in the Anglo-
Welsh canon: '*Edwards, to Barry-
John*' recited by Burton or Bassey,
as Bevan goes over in the corner

after eighteen sweet sherries.

"Effects of weathering on in situ dolerite & rhyolite outcrops from the Preseli Mountains, South Wales"

(Potts, Bernardini, Jones, et al. *X-Ray Spectrometry*, December 2005)


Exposure to the elements &
climate of Carn Menyn on
rock samples of rhyolite &
igneous spotted dolerite blue-

stones, reveals depletion rates
in surface concentrations of
calcium & yttrium consistent
with a steady state. Whilst

lead contents are markedly
increased due to emissions,
exhaust fumes & 'activities'
in step with ancient Britons

who hauled them down the A40
on their way to *Côr y Cewri**.

---

* 'Choir of Giants', the Welsh name for Stonehenge.

## NEOLITHIC

An erratic age brought raw materials
'as found', pre-cast, on a monumental
scale: concrete, vernacular, functional.

The exposed feature of a lintel slab
on the hard shoulder of an orthostat
or sarsen road by which it was dragged

at glacial speed. Saw an emphasis
on mass & void, geometrical solids
& roughcast, greywether surfaces –

fitness for purpose. A lithic machine
for living in. The hut circle dwellings
of a future city in ancient ruins, on

the brutalist model of one part sand
to two parts cement of Stone Age Man.

## The Foragers

A tribe of hunter-gatherers
is picking through our wheelie bins,
sifting our recycling boxes,
dipping into skips.
By the sodium light of a harvest moon
they are gleaning from the tip,
reaping what we've sown.


They collect in the ancient wood
with Tupperware & trugs,
wild garlic on their breath.
They know the countryside, its code:
rosehip, blackthorn, nettle, dock.
The eldest bites into a mushroom,
the youngest licks a frog.


A preagricultural society
*connecting with its food source*
in the wastes behind the Co-Op,
graingiver of stale crusts,
windfall of bruisefruit, &
from the midden all the trimmings
to roadkill left by the butcher's van.


They are 'freegans' if not vegans,
nor vegetarians either.
In the catchment of the omnivore:
the net, the trap, the burlap sack,
is wildfowl & wildflower,
flora in or out of season,
fauna past its sell-by date.


They are Jacks by the hedges,
poachers after eggs,
coarse anglers at the goldfish pond.
They go drifting to the tideline
for the catch of the day,
or dangle by their heels over
shrimp, samphire, sea purslane.

Twilight brings them back by
unknown roads, the pouches of their
cheeks & hoodies full of bane.
There are blood spoors in the lane,
splatters & squits
like mixed berry compotes
on the kerbstones of our doorsteps,


& in the underpass, cave drawings,
the scent of rut musk, rags-&-bones
– a whole mystery & mythos.
In the night sky before bin day,
in the fixed constellations
of our satellites & suburbs,
Orion stalks his prey.

Veganuary

After a month of meatless Mondays,
fish-free Fridays, nut roast Sundays,
plant-based only, eggs nor dairy,
ancient grains & acai berries,
super-, raw-, or wholefood bowls, &
drive-thru *Greggs* Quorn sausage rolls;
a 31-day ethical purge of
leather, feathers, silks & fur,
cashmere sweaters, wool-mix fibres,
beeswax, tallow, or bone china,
fresh 'n' clean of soap detergents,
toothpaste, medicines, antiperspirant
or antifreeze; re-wild & free,
flatulent with GHGs,
piebald, distended, spongiform
demented, rancid, gargety & gaunt
with rinderpest – on the 1$^{st}$ of Feb.
over the meadows
  the cows come home
    & trample us to death.

FLEXITARIAN

Under the glass vivarium,
transitioning the diets of
my non-traditional pets &
hothouse home companions

away from hyper-, obligate
carnivore to opportunistic,
via cruelty-free alternatives
& semi-, flexi-, surrogates:

cheat meats, pea protein prey,
warm-blooded pulses, fruit
surprise or veggie substitute
as part of our 5-a-day, I'm

enmeshed in their food webs,
stuck in the snake's deep throat,
down the exotic rabbit hole,
the pocket of my pocket pet,

my head in the unhinged mouth
of a dentate Venus flytrap,
besmeared in agave syrup
staked out on a termite mound.

IGNATIUS

*(2005 – 2022)*


Popes pious & infallible
play God & say that animals
have not immortal souls
nor shall enjoy eternal life,

but they can join Iscariot,
the cat bin woman & the vet,
in the last circle of hell. Sweet
boy, we grant you paradise.

## MIMIC

'Nor ever lived on earth a wiser bird'
OVID, *On the Death of His Mistress' Parrot*

Don't ask a little bird to tell you
*"Who's a pretty Polly?"* else you
end up talking to yourself. You

hear about these social species
with polyglot abilities &
thousand-word vocabularies, but

most of us are Trappist brothers
vowed to silence, Cosa Nostra,
cagey, or just can't be bothered.

Yet whilst we're on the subject, Pet
of tacit knowledge better left
unspoken & unsaid, never

leave me in the hands of strangers,
% the next-door neighbours'
son or daughter to feed & water

lest they forget & find me cold as
your sister's tit, carked it, croaked.
& who, in that familiar trope,

conceal the evidence in the bin,
the cat, around the U-bend, then
flush my faithful feathered friend

from the *rarae aves* in the tropic
regions of pet supermarkets,
the gumtrees of the internet, or

mist net of a pair of nylons among
the charms & pandemoniums of
feral suburban populations. Now

look in the budgie mirror, Pet:
same size, same body shape, right sex
dimorphic plumage – more or less.

My rosy-faced, yellow-collared,
variegated, multicoloured,
lesser-spotted & superb

accessory to the perfect murder,
in strict observance of omertà
but for the hubris of *hamartia*,

that preening, narcissistic flaw in
a best laid plan unbargained for
– after the fact, if not before – as

you hold me for further questioning,
over & over, again & again:
*"Who's a pretty Polly then?"* &

like a canary I sing. Sing. Si-i-i-i-i-i-i-i-ing.

## GIFT HORSE

Your unicorn arrived today,
I checked the manifest &
its mouth for signs of periodontal
gum & tooth defects.

It was then that I discovered
– conceive of my dismay –
its horn was no more
than a vulgar, plastic,
strap-on marital aid,
hanging rather limply
from a yard of packing tape.

*"It defies all trade description"*
said the Citizens Advice,
*"though it could be a carthorse*
*with a dildo of course,*
*riddled with ringworm & lice."*

& directed me
to the glue factory
where I led it by carrot & stick,
& they cemented the horn
of your unicorn
with a bond of permanent fix.

I brushed up its coat &
            combed out its mane,

fed it with horse pills,
            & syrup & maize,

rigged-up a rope-saddle,
            stirrup & reins,

& we joined a
            passing cavalcade

& rode through the city of love.

## RENTOKIL

A man most needful to this town
is the council pest
controller, so
you call the
Freefone number: *"For
vermin & Black Death... press #1"*.

You conjure up a Dickensian
ratoner in a coat of pelts,
a cricket bat
with a
nail in it & pye
dog at heel. Instead your

man rolls up in a van & armed
with clipboard & pen
makes a quick
inspection
of the garden, then
ticks the box marked: poison.

*Neosorexa Rodenticide* in fatal
– though humane –
dosages of bait
blocks at
feeding sites
& harbourages. You follow

his breadcrumb trail down to a
hole in the party wall,
set the trap,
brick it
up, come in &
wash your hands of it. Over

strong, sweet tea you ask his worst
fears: escaped tarantulas?
not-so-dwarf
crocodiles?
exotic dancing
snakes? The only thing, he

says, that gets to him are the
unfound 'body jobs',
& how a
starving
pet starts in at
the soft part of the cheek. You

wave him off from your plague-free
door as the angel of death
passes over
just one
of eighty houses he
visits each working week.

You only realise you've forgotten
to return his Customer
Satisfaction
Survey
the morning the
children go missing.

AGAPEMONE

*The Agapemonites were an Adventist self-sufficient community*
*& 'love cult' founded by the Reverend Henry Prince (1811-1899)*
*in the Somerset village of Spaxton, near Bridgwater.*


Put away we raiment, scorned we
those the sensual plains of Ely,
diocese of Bath & Wells, the see
        of Sodom by the Sea.

Relinquished we possessions for
a treasure laid in Heaven, &
on these Somersetshire levels
        builded we Beth-El.

A mission hall shaped as an ark
of covenant twixt Arts & Crafts,
wherein, behind steamed-up stained glass,
        privet & pampas grass,

didst dwell Himself in that Abode
of Love, that Agapæ of old, the
Passion of the Holy Ghost made
        mottled flesh below

in His Great Manifestation, as
like a rutting roe upon the
mount of Canticles, or Song of
        Songs of Solomon.

Thus, whilst we toiled in the field
& vineyard of His ministry, He
taught free Love & practiced freely
        on our wifery, the

Rising Sun of Righteousness with
healing in His wings athrob,
pan-sexual, poly-amorous – "O
        *Long Live Holy Love!*"

Left we His own begotten tribe the
Keys to earthly Paradise in the
fruit bowl, thence He this Life *yn*
        *twynkelyng of an iye.*

Him buried we in the garden in
the tuppenny position, east-
facing towards Spaxton-cum-
the-New-Jerusalem.

## AN HUSBANDMAN [EXCERPT FROM LITTLE DOMESDAY]

*As Fyftyeth Moste Elygyble*
*Bachelore I holde this*
*demesne as he afore me:*

*1 carucate of ploughelande,*
*as muche as one team canst*
*worke in a yeare & a daye;*

*wode for 4 swyne & 1 acre*
*of meadowe; an horse*
*in the homesteade; then 3*

*heade of cattle & afterwarde,*
*4; then 5 shepe, nowe 10;*
*of serfs the sayme number*

*as bordars & villeins; & then*
*– as nowe – 49 women.*

## CERTIFICATE OF BAD HUSBANDRY

Draft the mare & drove the old cow
from the byre that barely stands,
yoke them wife, & drive the plough

afield the furrow. Hoe & harrow,
scorch the earth & salt the ground
with leach & darnel. Let the milchcow

curdle, or go mad, the meadow
rewild, the dodder know no bounds,
the hedge into despondent slough

quickset & gate unhinge. The sow
in swine flu, & the hen egg-bound,
leave the theave & farrow cow

to foot-&-mouth or fairy arrow,
& me runoff, shitfaced in shamble-
dung, twixt *Barley Mow* & *Plough*.

By winter stubble, summer fallow,
common law & Stinted Land,
draft the mare & drove the old cow,
yoke them wife, & drive the plough.

ECLOGUE THE LAST

*No corpse of any person (except those who shall die of the plague)*
*shall be buried in any shift, sheet, or shroud, or anything*
*whatsoever made or mingled with flax, hair, gold, or silver, or in*
*any stuff, or thing, other than what is made of sheep's wool only.*

Act for Burying in Woollen, 1678

Fold me not by
the old wool book
in the parish chest,
the affidavit of
a Burial Act; &
fold me not by
hook or crook, in
sheepcote pritch,
the surplice slop
of a funeral shift,
a drabbet smock;
& fold me not in
linen, boxed in
flax, hemp, silk
or clothstuff, nap,
warp & woof of
sheet, or shroud;
but lay me in green
pastures down on
a hillside plot of
grazing land, to
shepherd's toft &
sheepman's croft;
thread-bare but
for forage crop, a
pair of odd argyll
socks & fingerless
mitt of the earnest
got; there to watch
upon my flock in
the pastoral care of
the Lamb of God.

## DOG PERSON

My biggest fear on becoming the wolfman
was not a full moon in the Lupus constellation.
Not the blood & gore, the banes & garlicks,
fleas & ticks & the worming tablets, the
catcher from the pound, or have-a-go hero,
nor the fact that in the sun I throw no shadow. No,
my biggest fear was getting older than my years
with progeria - or Hutchinson-Gilford syndrome -
not the tufts of hair on my shoulders, neck & ears,
but the age gap between us annually growing
at a man:dog ratio of one to seven.

& though to refute the philosopher's claim
that a dog can't be hopeful, I'll keenly await
your return on the morrow, or the following day,
be there with your slippers, the morning paper,
by then I'll be almost a fortnight older
yet in proportion none the wiser,
& it'll be too late to teach me new tricks
(fetch the *Andrex*, fly a Sputnik,
leap through burning hoops at Crufts)
or offer a sop to Cerberus.

So, seasonally adjust the daylight saving time,
synchronise the clocks & protect the sunshine,
check with the almanack for any metaphysical
event, plague of darkness, or total eclipse
of the '*kind, old sun*' by the lunatic moon,
mush to the pole of perpetual noon &
then rush back before the Evening Star
of civil dusk becomes the witching hour, &
in the way of these things a huntsman comes
with a silver bullet in his sunset gun.

## THE MANDRAKE

Vor the hourly rate of a minimum wage we
brung in the harras an baled the hay, pulled
up the beets, pixed the hops an the pears,
bunted the wheat from the chaff an the tare.

I war up in the top veel yarly un morning
cutting a swath thorough barleycorn whun
I skags on a nap that jist ooden buckle nor
budge to the edge of the sive or sickle. Za

I plants both feet an yanks by the roots as
ye dentist extracting a wisdom tooth, an the
piercing shriek as en tears from the ground
warn't animal, vegetable, but human sound,

thou b'ain't niver heard the like in yourn life
what a-rang in me ears as I runs for the wife.
Well, us wait till voke is abade then creaped
back up the heave wi' lanthorn an peak, sure

enough, he'm dade, as brickle as kexy, stiff
as a lath of thatch or pull-reed. Boy's Love
cries she, mawed down in he youth, zitch
a flower-like, nestle tripe blooth. Any road

whilst the lammas moon up on high an the
owls in they wood all turns a blind eye, we
lumpers he out to yon meadow an mores'n
aneen like a crossbeamed scarecrow. Ther'

ence we lay low in the lew of the land, wi'
us nose to the grindstone, ear to the ground,
yet norra un see'd nothing, nuther came vor'
ard wi' anonymous tip-offs of cereal murder.

Now us follows the seasonal work, migrates
thorough market town to farm estate, us're
childless still thauf her kneels an prays to
ye household gods an them crop deities, an

us borrid as pigs in the back of the van, or
unner the stars in the skeering land. Thauf
her dance round the maypole, an sacrifice
ourn wherewi' by the tenth an the tithe to

fertility drugs an IVF, whaur I banks my
seed, she abrood hern eggs, an turns ourn
quoins each new minted moon, I's firing
blanks, she'm as drow as the tomb. Us're

inbred, incestuous, wust – we's cursed by
that miserable sod I pulled from the yarth,
who'm thaur to this day, mommet hanged
like Christ a-crucified, yourn wicker man.

————————————————————

*harras* – harvest;
*bunted* – separated;
*yarly* – early;
*skags* – tears or rips;
*sive* – scythe;
*abade* – abed;
*heave* – hill;
*dade* – dead;
*kexy* – dried stalks;
*Boy's Love* – the herb Southernweed;
*zitch* – such;
*blooth* – blossom;
*mores* – roots in;
*ther'ence* – from that place;
*norra un* – not one;
*thauf* – though;
*skeering* – pastureland;
*abrood* – sit on, as a hen her eggs;
*drow* – dry, dusty;
*yarth* – earth;

*pixed* – picked;
*veel* – field;
*thorough* – through;
*nap* – knoll;
*voke* – folk;
*creaped* – crept;
*peak* – pitchfork;
*brickle* – brittle;
*pull-reed* – pond reed, for thatching;
*mawed* – mowed;
*nestle tripe* – puny runt;
*lumper* – carry heavily;
*aneen* – upright;
*lew* – shelter;
*nuther* – neither;
*borrid* – lustful;
*wherewi'* – goods, money;
*quoins* – coins;
*wust* – worst;
*mommet* – scarecrow.

## Pete Marsh

'…*but thrust their buried men back in the human mind again.*'
                                W B Yeats, *Under Ben Bulben*


Should a Lindow man find a Lindow Man in a peat bog
                                2,000 years from now,

don't be surprised if he's a sacrifice straight from the pages
                                of *The Golden Bough,*

or sphagnum moss of some Law of Sod, offered to appease
                                a fertility goddess

judging by the presence of mistletoe pollens found in the
                                contents of the stomach.



Whose tannin-stained, earthborn remains bear witness to
                                an untimely end: a

broken neck & blow to the head with an Iron Age blunt
                                instrument, then

finally drowned, & buried here face down on a tribal
                                boundary in line

with tradition, or upright position within easy walking
                                distance of the sea.

When the Crime Scene Investigation team dusts me for
                                        genetic fingerprints,

& I'm bubble wrapped & Jiffy bagged to the lab for
                                        further analysis, where

they carbon date me, then marinate me in a vat of
                                        polyethylene glycol,

before CT-scanning & 3D-mapping a tomographic
                                        image of the skull.


An artist's impression of a national treasure, exhibited on
                                        permanent display in

the Mummy Room of the British Museum, as *luz* or Lazarus
                                        by any other name. No,

don't be surprised – mortified – if such morbid anatomy &
                                        forensic research, dig

up pathologically & archaeologically the one thing you'd
                                        rather left unearthed.

## ALLOTMENT

Then plant me out & bed me down in
one man's lot of plotted ground,
& let me run to seed

where loam feet make a rod or perch,
& four square make a daywork, &
three score years & ten of earth
a sowing, scatter me

in the midst of must & matter, mould
& litter, lay me down to mulch
in back-to-basic peace

on that small hold of new beginnings,
comings, goings, "earlys", ends,
among the cut-&-come-agains
O let me run to seed.

*we are risen from creation*
  *myth & mystery religion*

*in weather lore & cycle of*
  *the grain we are born again*

*as gods who lay all winter*
  *long in that other kingdom*

*of fallow field & foulmere*
  *fen we are the resurrection*

*whispered in the seedtime*
  *the plant miracle of spring*

*ascending in due season*
  *to the land of the living*

*& the countryside beyond*
  *we are risen   we are risen*

# Acknowledgements

Acknowledgements are due to the editors of the following publications in which a number of these poems, or versions thereof, first appeared: *Ambit*; *Brittle Star*; *Dreich*; *The Journal*; *Magma*; *Poetry News*; *Poetry Salzburg Review* & *Popshot Quarterly*.

'Saturnian' was first posted on the Science Museum website on National Poetry Day 2021.

'"Effects of weathering on in situ dolerite & rhyolite outcrops from the Preseli Mountains, South Wales"' takes its title from the magazine article cited & was published in the anthology pamphlet: *Poems from Pembrokeshire* (Seren, March 2019).

'In Response to Delabole Slate' was included in *The Echoing Gallery: Bristol Poets & Art in the City* anthology (Redcliffe Press, 2013).

'Recently Discovered Fragment from Coleridge's Lost Notebook' was commissioned by the Bristol University *'Romantic Bristol: Writing the City'* collaborative digital project (June 2016).

Two of these poems originally appeared in the pamphlet collection: *Field Trips in the Anthropocene* (Rack Press, 2020). Reprinted by kind permission.

Two of these poems originally appeared in the pamphlet collection: *The Encyclopædist* (Melos Press, 2016). Reprinted by kind permission.

I am grateful to Lee Hutchinson, Curator of History, M Shed, Bristol, for his assistance with the cover image.

My personal thanks to Rachael Boast, Nicholas Murray, William Palmer, Ian Pople, Lucy Tunstall, Michael Vince & Amy Wack.

& forever indebted to Melissa Bevan.